BEACON SERMON OUTLINE SERIES

SERMON OUTLINES
— ON —

The Life &
Teachings
of Christ

GENE WILLIAMS

Beacon Hill Press of Kansas City
Kansas City, Missouri

Copyright 2003 by
Beacon Hill Press of Kansas City

ISBN 083-412-0631

Printed in the
United States of America

Cover Design: Paul Franitza

Library of Congress Cataloging-in-Publication Data

Williams, Gene, 1932-
    Sermon outlines on the life and teachings of Christ / Gene Williams.
        p. cm. — (Beacon sermon outline series)
    ISBN 0-8341-2063-1 (pbk.)
    1. Jesus Christ—Biography—Sermons—Outlines, syllabi, etc. 2. Jesus Christ—Teachings—Sermons—Outlines, syllabi, etc.. I. Title. II. Series.

    BT306.33.W55 2003
    251'.02—dc21

                                                                    2003009638

10 9 8 7 6 5 4 3 2 1

Contents

Introduction

Messages from the
Life and Teachings of Jesus

The sermon outlines in this volume come from the life and teachings of Jesus. Some of the messages have their roots in who and how He was. He was the divine Son of God, who came to let us know that the awesome Creator of the universe still loves us.

In order for us to fully receive that message, Jesus did some wonderful things. For example, He performed 33 miracles for the benefit of the people.

Some of these messages will focus on the simple but powerful words He uttered. The truths He taught may be more important than the physical miracles He performed. Jesus took the marvelous lessons about the Creator-Father and made them so simple that anyone could understand them. In preaching these outlines everyone who hears them will better understand the beautiful truth that our Heavenly Father loves us and wants to have fellowship with us.

There are also some outlines in this series on the nature of Jesus. What was He like? What does that mean to me? These messages help us to better understand how loving and kind Jesus was and still is today. Focusing the minds of our people on Jesus can only result in one thing. He said, "But I, when I am lifted up from the earth, will draw all men to myself" (John 12:32). People whose minds are focused on Jesus are drawn and driven. They are drawn into His presence and driven by His purpose.

When these sermon seeds are mixed with faith, prayer, and your fertile minds, something wonderful will come forth.

Meet the Christ

John 1:14-27

Introduction

A. When Jesus came into the world, He brought with Him a living certainty. Everything connected with Him spoke of a message in which people could believe.
   1. This confidence began with His coming into the world.
      a. The angels told Joseph, "You are to give him the name Jesus, because he *will* save his people from their sins" (Matt. 1:21*b*, emphasis added).
      b. The angels told the shepherds, "A Savior has been born to you; he *is* Christ the Lord" (Luke 2:11*b*, emphasis added).
      c. The sainted Simeon said, "My eyes *have seen* your salvation" (Luke 2:30, emphasis added).
   2. The testimony of the apostles proclaimed this confidence (Acts 2:36; 16:31).
B. The advent of Jesus was divine certainty among the confusion of humankind.
C. Read the scripture: John 1:14-27.
D. The confusion in today's world could be solved by accepting Jesus' message.

I. John the Baptist's Announcement Offered Hope (vv. 24-27)

A. Note the pathos in John's proclamation as he says, "Among you stands one you do not know" (v. 26*b*).
   1. They had looked and longed for Him to come but still did not realize that He already had.
   2. Could this be a reflection of our world today—people looking for a Messiah who has already come?
   3. Look at the religious people of John's day.
      a. They were concerned about sin and religious orthodoxy.
      b. They were a pathetic people wandering in a spiri-

7

tual wilderness as they awaited the coming of the Messiah.

  B. John made the announcement that had been awaited for centuries.

    1. The answer to sin has come (v. 29)!

    2. A solution to their major problem, sin, was available.

  C. The message John gave to his world is available for our world today.

    1. It says to us that there is a solution to our sin problem.

    2. Remember the message of Rev. 3:20.

II. John the Baptist Dispelled Any Confusion That Might Exist (John 1:19-23).

  A. His pride could have been appealed to by the question in verse 21.

    1. Note that John knew who he was and what his assignment was (v. 23).

    2. He gave a clear-cut testimony that dispelled any doubt or confusion.

  B. The world in which we live is looking for solid answers.

    1. People wonder whom they can trust for leadership to make the most of their lives.

    2. Some religious bodies have been know to confuse rather than clarify this issue.

  C. All other religious groups must admit that they are not the final authority for a relationship with God.

    1. John's finger points directly to Jesus Christ (v. 27).

    2. John had a clear understanding of his relationship with his Lord (v. 27).

III. John the Disciple's Message Promised Victory (vv. 14-18)

  A. The key to certain and complete victory is a relationship with Jesus Christ.

    1. Nothing else that people trust (money, popularity, and power) can provide this.

    2. The message that John gives us provides confidence and assurance in abundance.

  B. John's message is a great revelation.

    1. The dim word of prophecy became bright when the Word became flesh.

2. The grace to live victoriously has been revealed in Christ.
C. The victory that comes from Jesus is the victory of grace (v. 17).
    1. Jesus gives blessing after blessing after blessing. "From the fullness of his grace we have all received one blessing after another" (v. 16).
    2. The Amplified Bible reads, "For out of His fullness (abundance) we all received—all had a share and we were all supplied with—one grace after another and spiritual blessing upon spiritual blessing, and even favor upon favor."

Conclusion

A. John the Baptist cleared up any confusion or doubt they may have had.
B. Jesus Christ is the key to a personal relationship with God.
C. You, too, can know Him personally.

JESUS

Matthew 1:21

Introduction

A. In biblical days the names given to children were significant. Parents chose names in anticipation of the lives of
their children. Look at some significant names: Jacob—
may God protect; Isaiah—God is salvation; David—
beloved or chieftain; Joshua—savior or deliverer.

B. Jesus is the most significant of all names that were given
to biblical children. When the angel directed Joseph to
name Mary's child Jesus, it was clear what that Child's life
was to become. Read the scripture: Matt. 1:21.

C. To many people Jesus is just another word, but it is
deeply significant. An examination of each letter will en-
hance our understanding of this significance.

I. The First Letter Is *J* and Stands for Justification

A. The penalty of death was upon all of the descendants of
Adam and Eve.
1. Animals were used to make installments on the debt
of sin. A highly organized plan is laid out in Leviticus.
2. The priest, using the blood of innocent animals,
sought forgiveness for sins.

B. Jesus came to end animal sacrifices (Heb. 9:11-14).
1. He is the Lamb of God (John 1:29, 36).
2. Jesus became our great High Priest (Heb. 10:11-12).

C. Jesus means that we are justified before God and can
face Him without shame.

II. The Second Letter Is *E* and Stands for Eternal Life

A. Every soul spends eternity somewhere. This is a universal
belief by people even in many places where the Bible has
never been preached.

B. Jesus' coming means that eternal life is offered to everyone (John 3:16).

C. There are many questions about eternity that cannot be answered. A wise person knows to be prepared for it.

III. The Third Letter Is *S* and Stands for Salvation

A. We do not have to wait for eternity to realize Jesus' blessings.
   1. John 10:10 promises an abundant life now.
   2. In the New Testament the lives of everyone Jesus touched were changed.
B. Genuine Christians enjoy life at its best now. Every person in our world who has a personal encounter with Jesus is raised to a new level of living.
C. The salvation offered by Jesus means the best things that life has to offer now.

IV. The Fourth Letter Is *U* and Stands for Unlimited Grace

A. Jesus brings hope for every human being.
   1. Every person can be saved from sin (John 3:16).
   2. He does not want anyone to perish (2 Pet. 3:9).
   3. He came to seek and save all who are lost (Luke 19:10).
B. People get mired deeply in sin and need to be delivered.
   1. David discovered God's delivering grace (Ps. 40:1-3).
   2. Mary Magdalene had been delivered from deep sin (Luke 8:2).
   3. Romans 5:8 promises deliverance.
C. Since there are no new sins, we can be sure His grace can change us as well.

V. The Final Letter *S* Stands for Security

A. It is one thing to get saved; it is another to stay saved. Jesus prayed for our keeping grace in John 17.
B. It also means security in every other aspect of our lives. There is nothing that can ever come into our lives for which Jesus is not sufficient.

Conclusion

A. Jesus is the world's most significant name.
B. He justifies, He gives eternal life, He saves us now, He reaches to every person, and He makes us secure in himself.
C. Do you know Jesus for who He really is?

Jesus Revealed

John 1:29-34

Introduction

    A. Many people have difficulty getting a clear, undistorted picture of Jesus. They know about Him, but they do not know Him. There are many mistaken ideas about what He was like.

    B. John the Baptist endeavored to help those listening to him get a clear view of who Jesus really was. Read the scripture: John 1:29-34. John told them, "Behold, perceive, look at clearly, consider from every angle." Those people who took the time to look at Jesus found their lives changed forever. The same can be true today.

I. To Whom Was John Calling the Attention of the People?

    A. Jesus Christ of Nazareth

        1. Son of the Holy Spirit and Mary

        2. Son of Joseph the carpenter, His adopted earthly father

    B. Let's take a look at the historical Christ.

        1. He was a very real person in history.

        2. Even people who refuse to accept the authenticity of the Bible must acknowledge the historical evidence of Jesus.

        3. Jesus is historically provable. A single trip to Israel will remove all doubt.

    C. We need to see Christ as more than a person in history.

        1. John the Baptist pointed to the Lamb of God who came to solve the sin problem.

        2. John, the disciple and author of this gospel, emphasized the divine nature of Jesus. In 1:1-4 Jesus is presented as eternally existent with the Father. In 3:16 we are told that Jesus was sent from the Father. In chapter 17 Jesus prayed to His Heavenly Father.

    D. Jesus wanted there to be no mistake about His true nature (Matt. 16:13-20). That is why the disciples followed Him at great personal sacrifice.

E. Who do you think Jesus Christ really is? Today, too many believe solely in the historical Jesus. We need to know Jesus personally as the divine Son of God.

II. Why Is Believing in Jesus So Essential?

A. Jesus did many things during His lifetime.
 1. It is easy to focus on the sideline activities, such as the miracles He performed.
 2. John the Baptist called attention to the main purpose of Jesus' coming—-our redemption (John 1:29).
 3. We must not allow Jesus' supreme sacrifice to get lost in the busyness of life.

B. The use of the designation "Lamb" was significant.
 1. This reminded the Jews of the Passover and their deliverance from bondage.
 2. It shows that Jesus is our Lamb of deliverance from the greater bondage of sin.

III. Jesus Is the Answer to Life

A. The people who lived in John's day needed help. They were looking for a spiritual leader. That is why they had gone to him (1:19).
 1. John rejected the ego-satisfying opportunity of the occasion (v. 21).
 2. He knew that Jesus alone is the answer (vv. 26-27).

B. Today, people still need help.
 1. Interest in religion is increasing because of the spiritual hunger in all people.
 2. It is not enough just to be religious.
 3. Many spiritually oriented movements are trying to fill the empty void in people.

C. Jesus is the only answer to fulfilling the spiritual needs of human beings.

Conclusion

A. Give personal testimony of how Jesus transformed your life.

B. I challenge you today to behold the historical God-Man who is the answer to life.

The Incomparable Christ

Luke 9:28-36

Introduction

The experience in today's passage that took place on the top of the Mount of Transfiguration provides the basis for the desperately needed truth—Jesus has no equal. Read the scripture: Luke 9:28-36. On that special occasion those who knew Jesus best were presented with the unquestionable truth that Jesus is the Son of God. Peter had committed the error that is made by many today of assuming the equality of religious leaders (v. 33*b*). God wanted there to be no mistake about the uniqueness of His Son (v. 35). We need a clear, undistorted view of who Jesus Christ really is.

I. Across the Centuries There Have Been Many Great People of God

A. Abraham, the father of Israel

He was a man of such faith that he was committed to God's will even to the point of being willing to sacrifice his only son. There is nothing wrong with Abraham (see Heb. 11:8-19).

B. David, favorite king of Israel

As a man of faith he defeated Goliath, an overwhelming enemy (1 Sam. 17). We would be pleased to have a leader like David in our lives today.

C. There are many other great people of God, such as Isaiah, Daniel, Ezekiel, and so on.

D. Two men who had great impacts on Israel were present at the Transfiguration.

1. Moses had been God's instrument for the deliverance of his people from bondage. He had been inspired by God to write the story of earth's beginnings. He was entrusted with the law for humankind's standards for living. At the Transfiguration God was telling us that Jesus is the greatest Deliverer and has the message to guide us to deliverance.

2. Elijah had been such a powerful prophet of God that King Ahab feared him. By faith he accomplished what 450 prophets of Baal could not (1 Kings 18). God wanted us to know that Jesus goes beyond striking fear in the hearts of those who are evil. He won the ultimate battle on Calvary.

E. When God had these two great men join Him on the mountaintop, He still made it clear that Jesus stands alone. There is no one worthy of comparison with Him.

II. Is There Any Other Hope?

A. There are many religions in the world today with great numbers of followers. These include Confucianism, Shintoism, Islam, Hinduism, and Buddhism. None of these compare to the high calling of God in Christ Jesus.

B. The Word is very clear: "Salvation is found in no one else, for there is no other name under heaven given to men by which we must be saved" (Acts 4:12).

III. Jesus Is Totally Incomparable

A. He was born as no other person. The *how* of Jesus' virgin birth becomes believable when the *who* is remembered.

B. He lived as no one else. His contemporaries had to acknowledge Him to be the Son of God (Matt. 14:33).

C. His death and resurrection are unique in history.

Conclusion

A. Illustration: The story is told of a brilliant Brahman scholar in India who was disturbed about the progress of Christianity among his people. He planned to distribute a pamphlet that would expose the weaknesses of Jesus. He spent 11 years searching and became convinced that Jesus is all the Bible said He is and was converted.

B. A similar experience awaits all who take time to look at the incomparable Christ.

The Incomparable Christ—His Compassion

Luke 19:28-41

Introduction

    A. Jesus lived 33 years, during which time He shaped the course of history.

        1. Many people have shone with brilliance for brief periods of time. But they have all burned out and faded away. Jesus continues to shine.

        2. Occasionally a meteorite will race through our solar system, burn brightly for a while, and may even rival the sun in its brightness. But it ultimately disappears, while the sun continues to dominate our universe.

        3. This is the same way with Jesus. He stands alone as the ultimate positive power.

    B. Jesus stands alone because of two great qualities that exist in Him as in no other person who has ever lived—His compassion; His power. This Sunday and next week we will look at these two aspects of Jesus. Read the scripture: Luke 19:28-41.

I. Jesus Could Have Been King

    A. Look at the incident in the Scriptures that is recorded in all four Gospels.

        1. See Matt. 21, Mark 11, Luke 19, and John 12. This was the only hour of celebration in His life on earth. They wanted to make Him a king. He refused (John 6). According to today's passage, Jesus had to be recognized at that time.

        2. In His triumphal entry Jesus gave them what they needed. The people needed a song, and Jesus gave them "Hosanna!" Music and Jesus are inseparable. His people are a joyful, happy crowd.

    B. Even in that Triumphal Entry, Jesus was compassionate.

        1. In Matt. 21:5 we read a quote from Zech. 9:9. It is a command to rejoice.

        2. While Jesus came in the traditional manner of a king,

He did not come with an army in power. He came with peasants raising their voices in praise.

    3. This incident displayed Jesus' triumph of humility over pride, and meekness and gentleness over rage and anger.

II. The Life of Jesus Was Filled with Compassion

A. Jesus wept over the city of Jerusalem (Luke 19:41).
1. He knew what was coming, and His heart ached for them (vv. 43-44).
2. He had compassion for the crowd (14:14).
3. This is a clear message from God that He has compassion for everyone.

B. Jesus wept over individuals.
1. He had concern for a leper for whom no one else cared. No one is excluded. Jesus cares for everyone (Mark 1:40-42).
2. He felt compassion for a poor widow who lost her only son. She did not ask for help. Jesus saw her need and was moved with compassion (Luke 7:13).
3. While His compassion is broad enough to include everyone, it is narrow enough to concentrate on each one.
4. Sometimes we must cry out to get help as the two blind men near Jericho did (Matt. 20:30). Jesus always responds to a cry for help.

C. There have been many people who were meek, kind, sensitive souls. But no one has ever lived who can compare with Christ.

Conclusion

A. When we remember Jesus' triumphal entry as a king, we must also remember the compassion that carried Him through the city and on to the Cross.
1. On the Cross Jesus met humankind's greatest need—forgiveness for sins.
2. Nothing and no one can ever compare with that.

B. If possible, close with the hymn "No One Ever Cared for Me Like Jesus."

The Incomparable Experience That Jesus Brings

John 9:1-7, 18-25

Introduction

A. We have been looking at the fact that no one compares to Jesus. He occupies an incomparable position before God—historical but divine. He is incomparable among all people who have ever lived. He is incomparable as a teacher. He taught us how to live as no one else.

B. Today, we are going to look at the incomparable change He makes in lives. Read John 9:1-7; 18-25. It is good news to know that while we live in unsettled times, there is one thing of which we can be certain. Jesus Christ can enable us to live the life God intended.

I. Let's Take a Look at the Story in Today's Scripture

A. The man in this passage had a serious problem. He had been born blind.

1. His blindness was no one's fault (v. 3). Sometimes we need to quit looking for something to blame for our difficulties. We are human. Human beings have frailties and defects.

2. This man's need is like that of many in our world today. He could not fully appreciate life. No one does until there is a personal relationship with Jesus.

B. The story in this passage raises a lot of questions. No one understood what had happened to him. People even had difficulty agreeing about who this man was. The world still does not understand the change that takes place in the lives of those who have been genuinely born again.

C. They could not understand how the miracle happened. The man did not understand (vv. 15-16). His parents did not understand (vv. 20-21). The Pharisees questioned him, but nothing changed his response (vv. 24-25).

D. He had total confidence in the miracle in the midst of their confusion (v. 25). Note in verse 25 his personal knowledge of the results of Jesus' touch. Nothing could break down a personal encounter with Jesus Christ.

II. The Results of an Encounter with Jesus Are Still Unquestionable

A. Many things in our world are questionable.
   1. What people believe to be important today may be gone tomorrow.
   2. This results in the frustration so many people experience. They have nothing about which they can be certain.
   3. Solomon testified to the emptiness of the world's provision (Eccles. 2:1-12).
B. The question that all of us must face is, "What is there in our lives about which we can be sure?" The world does not understand the changes that take place in our lives when we come to know Jesus.

Conclusion

A. There will always be some questions about some of the things that are going on in our lives.
   1. We will always be curious about why certain tragedies and events happen to us.
   2. Like the disciples who asked, "Who sinned that this man was born blind?" (see John 9:2), we want to fix the blame. But sometimes there is no blame. Things just happen.
B. In the midst of all of life's uncertainties, there is one thing about which that we can be absolutely certain—that our lives have been touched by Jesus and as the result a change has taken place.
C. If you were physically blind and offered the opportunity to see, how long would you wait? Spiritual blindness is more critical than being unable to see.
D. Jesus wants to give you the incomparable experience that will open your spiritual eyes and totally change your life.

The Incomparable Christ—His Power

Luke 24:1-8

Introduction

   A. Jesus Christ has had many rivals, but there has been no equal to Him as the most influential person who ever lived and walked on earth.

   B. Last week we considered Jesus' compassion.

   C. It is important to note that compassion without power accomplishes very little of lasting value.

      1. To be what humankind really needs we must not only care but also have the power to make a difference in each situation.

      2. It is true that power without compassion becomes tyranny and is unsatisfactory.

      3. Compassion without power to act provides very little help

      4. Jesus' display of power in our scripture makes Him incomparable with anyone else. Read Luke 24:1-8.

I. Jesus Exhibited His Power in Many Ways

   A. His power is displayed in His miracles.

      1. In John 2 His compassion for the young bridegroom was mixed with His power to change things.

      2. In Mark 4:35-31 Jesus was concerned for the disciples' safety and calmed the storm.

      3. In John 5 He felt compassion for a helpless man and changed his life forever.

      4. In John 6 He had compassion on a hungry multitude and fed them.

      5. In all, Jesus performed 33 miracles where He mixed compassion and power to change the lives of people.

   B. He exhibited power in the restraint He displayed in the final hours of His life.

   C. The power of Jesus' love lifted people to new heights of living.

1. In John 4 He changed the life of the woman at the well.
2. He changed Matthew's life (Matt. 9).
3. He changed the life of a Pharisee named Saul into that of a powerful apostle (Acts 9).
   D. The power to change human lives is greater than any of the other miracles.

II. Jesus' Most Astounding Display of Power Is the Resurrection

A. This fact is the heart and core of Christianity, and it is justifiably so.
1. Paul wrote, "And if Christ has not been raised, our preaching is useless and so is our faith" (1 Cor. 15:14).
2. The Resurrection is the confirmation of all that we believe about Jesus.
3. Illustration: A car without a motor is useless. In the same way, everything in the New Testament is void without Jesus' resurrection.

B. What about the Resurrection?
1. It is not a myth or stereotypical story that has been passed down by devout people who accepted the Resurrection without reason.
2. Common sense teaches that if the story of the Resurrection could be justifiably and scientifically discredited, Jesus' enemies would do just that.
3. The priests were afraid of the possibility of the Resurrection (Matt. 27:62-66).
4. Their acts helped verify the validity of Jesus' resurrection.

C. For a period of more than 40 days Jesus was seen on at least 10 occasions. Those sightings happened in many situations (1 Cor. 15:3-8). In any court of law such evidence would constitute a confirmation of the fact.

Conclusion

A. Jesus Christ came with incomparable compassion but exhibited incomparable power that has brought about a change in the lives of all that believe in Him.
B. The power of the Resurrection gives hope and confidence to all of us.

This Man Receives Sinners

Luke 15:1-24

Introduction

A. Luke 15 is one of the most valuable chapters in God's Word.
   1. It has been referred to as "the gospel in the gospels."
   2. The original audience was a group of indignant scribes and Pharisees.
   3. This chapter has three separate parables, but all of them have a common theme—God's compassion for the lost. These parables present a picture of God.

B. The first picture is of the Good Shepherd. Read verses 3-7.
   1. Sheep represented the major means of support for many Jews in that day.
   2. The sheep were wayward and defenseless. They needed constant supervision.
   3. The parable pictures the care of God for wayward people.

C. The second picture is of the woman who lost a coin. Read verses 8-10.
   1. It was a small coin of little value.
   2. It was important enough to that woman that she searched diligently and rejoiced when she found it.
   3. We may feel unimportant, but our Father earnestly searches for each one of us.

D. The third picture is of the lost son. Read verses 11-24.
   1. The young man in this parable rebelled against his father to his own peril.
   2. After tasting the fruit of sin, he realized his folly and returned to be a servant.
   3. God wants us to know that His arms are open to all who repent and return to Him.

E. Jesus used these three pictures to show why He "receives sinners" (vv. 1-2).

1. Every human being is of equal value to Him.
2. Jesus never denied the charge that He received sinners.

I. The Parables Picture Lost Humanity

A. In these parables Jesus teaches that people without God are lost.
   1. Jesus never called them "sinners." He called them "lost."
   2. They were lost to the presence, protection, and provision of their Heavenly Father.
B. Some people are lost in the same way the sheep was lost.
   1. The sheep did not deliberately run away. It simply wandered off.
   2. Some people are like that. They simply edge away, step-by-step.
C. Some people are lost in the same way the coin was lost.
   1. The carelessness of someone else contributed to the problem.
   2. Many people have difficulty in their lives because of the failings of others.
D. Some people are lost in the same way the son was lost.
   1. He left with full awareness of what he was doing.
   2. He had no one to blame but himself for the difficulty in which he found himself.

II. The Parables Reflect God's Attitude Toward Lost Humanity

A. The lesson of these parables is that our Father wants to have fellowship with all people regardless of what they have done. Illustration: Like the prodigal son, many people today are living beneath their privilege.
B. It is one thing to accept sinners. It is another thing to go looking for them.
   1. The first two parables clearly teach a seeking God.
   2. In these parables there is rejoicing when the lost are found.
   3. Jesus said, "I tell you, there is rejoicing in the presence of the angels of God over one sinner who repents" (v. 10).

III. The Parables Proclaim the Joy of Restoration

  A. In the parable of the prodigal, the son was throwing his life away until he returned.
   1. His experience in the pigpen was the lowest place imaginable to a Jew.
   2. When he came to himself and returned to his father, there was a great celebration.
  B. When the woman found the lost coin, she had a great time of rejoicing.
  C. When the shepherd found the lost sheep, he celebrated.
  D. All of these parables teach us that God longs to have fellowship with us.

Conclusion

  A. Jesus is assuring us that He receives sinners—they are important to Him. He searches for the lost and stands ready to receive anyone who returns to Him.
  B. Give your personal testimony. "I am glad Jesus receives sinners. He received me one day. He will do the same for you."

The Mind of Christ

Philippians 2:5-11

Introduction
A. Wouldn't it be wonderful if Christians acted like Jesus?
  1. The name "Christian" implies that we reflect Christ in our lives and natures.
  2. Christians are followers and imitators of Jesus Christ.
B. Paul admonished the church at Philippi to imitate the Master. This was a good church—-one of the best. Still, Paul felt the need to tell them of his concern that they follow Jesus. Read Phil. 2:5-11.
C. Our attitudes should be the same as that of Jesus Christ (v. 5). This Epistle shows some evidence of discord in that church. Paul wrote to correct that discord to keep that church in good spiritual condition. The text we have read is the central thought of the Epistle but is good advice for any church.

I. Christ's Mind Is Filled with Compassion
A. Whatever a person's spiritual condition may be, when asked about Jesus he or she always responds that He is love, compassion, and meekness.
B. Look at Jesus' attitude toward others. He always reached out to help anyone who would respond to Him. He was never too weary to help those who came to Him. He was never harsh or critical of those who came to Him for help. He recognized and allowed for the weakness of humanity.
C. Paul writes that we are to be like the compassionate Christ. According to verse 3, we are not to insist upon having our own way. According to verse 4, we are admonished to do everything we can to help others. "Don't just think about your own affairs, but be interested in others, too, and in what they are doing" (TLB). The mind of Christ reflected compassion. So must we.

II. The Mind of Christ Is Filled with Concern

A. Concern is closely akin to compassion, but there is a difference. Genuine compassion breaks forth into concern that leads to action.

B. Jesus illustrates this relationship in His caring for humankind and His acting upon that by sacrificing His life.

   1. Jesus acknowledged that we needed help and agreed to pay the price (vv. 6-8)
   2. Jesus was in heaven with the Father. He left heaven to come to earth to experience the pain of humanity.
   3. He demonstrated His concern for us by paying the ultimate price on the Cross.

C. Paul was writing that we need that same mind-set.

   The mind of Christ does not demand convenience or comfort. The world needs to see concerned Christians who will go out of their way to make a difference in their world. Illustration: The story of the Good Samaritan illustrates concern (Luke 10).

III. Christ's Mind Is One of Commitment

A. When compassion and concern are combined, commitment is the result.

B. Jesus was committed to the salvation of humankind. Although Jesus owed humanity nothing, compassion and concern caused Him to lay His life on the line. Jesus paid the price. He has given us the opportunity to be saved. Jesus was willing to do whatever it took for the benefit of human beings. Christians are to be committed to making a difference just as Christ has done. Illustration: Paul was a living example of the committed mind as He became a missionary and took the gospel everywhere he went.

Conclusion

A. Jesus did not come so that God would exalt Him. He came because He cared.

B. Paul was telling the Church to be like Jesus, to carry a burden, and to let that burden affect their lives.

C. Every person who has experienced the mind of Christ enjoys a great relationship with God.

The Changeless Christ

Hebrews 13:1-15

Introduction

    A. Whatever Jesus Christ ever was, He still is today. He was the Son of God. He remains the only begotten Son of God. He was the Prince of Peace. He still is the only sure way to personal peace. He was the great Healer. On occasions He still performs marvelous miracles. He was the Healer of broken hearts. He is still able to pick up the pieces of shattered lives and provide a reason to live. He was the Savior of the world, who died on the Cross. He is still our access for the total forgiveness of our sins.

    B. All that Jesus ever was, the Word promises He still is, and—better yet—He will be tomorrow. Read the scripture: Heb. 13:1-15.

I. Our World Has Bombarded Us with Changes

    A. The physical way we live has undergone drastic changes. We have gone from homes that had very few conveniences to those with every conceivable type of appliance. Our mode of travel has gone from horses to the jet age. Communication has gone from Morse code to the computer age.

    B. The code of conduct for our society has undergone tragic changes. Standards of conduct have been lowered to make people more comfortable in their sins. Sexual promiscuity has been rationalized as being normal.

    C. The Church has been victimized by these changes.

        1. In many cases we have become more interested in pleasing people than in challenging them to uphold a standard of holy living.

        2. Sometimes we are more focused on meeting people where they are than in taking them to where they need to be spiritually.

    D. There are some things that have not changed.

1. We must still be born again to enter the Kingdom of Heaven (John 3).
2. It still takes a pure heart to see God (Matt. 5:8).
3. It still takes obedience to the Father's will to enjoy His presence (7:21).

II. Look at Our Christ Who Has Not Changed

A. Jesus was always present at the point of need. He was with the Hebrew children in the fiery furnace (Dan. 3). He was with the frightened disciples on the storm on the sea (Matt. 14). He comforted brokenhearted worshipers on the road to Emmaus (Luke 24:13).

B. He was all-powerful and Master of every situation. He multiplied fish and bread to feed the hungry (John 6). He healed a man who had been helpless for 38 years (chap. 5). He raised Lazarus from the dead (chap. 11).

C. He felt compassion for the people. He cared for children even when He was weary (Luke 18:16). He shared the pain of the brokenhearted widow (7:11-17).

D. However, all of these events took place yesterday.

III. Jesus Christ Is Everything Today That He Ever Has Been

A. While it is wonderful to read what Jesus was like, it is more encouraging to know He is still the same today.
1. Just to know that He ever lived lifts our spirits.
2. To know that He still lives gives us courage and hope.

B. All that He ever was, He still is.

Conclusion

A. The best news of all is that what He was and is, He will be tomorrow. While the events of tomorrow are unpredictable, the outcome is not. The changeless Christ brings stability to our lives. Illustration: The great ships that sail our seas have an instrument called a Gyrostabilizer that ensures they are always level.

B. In geometry there are certain laws that never change. These provide the basis for the solution of many complicated problems.

C. We can count on Jesus Christ to take care of every situation in our lives.

The Understanding Christ

Matthew 19:13-15

Introduction

A. This passage of scripture gives us real insights into the nature of Jesus.

1. He had been traveling daily and constantly surrounded by people (vv. 1-2). He must have been physically weary.
2. He was frustrated with the Pharisees' nit-picking (v. 3).
3. The disciples knew what He had been through. So when the mothers brought their children to Jesus, the disciples decided to protect Him from the people.
4. Jesus understood the desires of those mothers. Regardless of how He felt physically or mentally, He responded to their needs.
5. Read the scripture: Matt. 19:13-15.

B. Jesus must have been a strong man physically. The rigors of the life He lived and the strong men who were drawn to Him give evidence that He was strong. When we add to His physical capabilities a sensitive, caring heart, the picture of Jesus is beautiful and inspiring. It is good to realize that Jesus had both sensitivity and physical ability. Today, we are looking at how well He understands people.

I. Jesus Understood the Minds of Humankind

A. He could have spoken in the clouded language of theologians. He knew that common people could not relate to that language and wanted everyone to have the opportunity to understand God. It is significant that the first people He called were simple fishermen. He had the ability to relate truths of splendor to simple minds. Remember, He could speak the language of scholars. Illustration: At age 12 He taught in the Temple (Luke 2:41-50).

B. Jesus still relates to us in this manner today. The things that matter most are simple. He communicates with us in a way that we can comprehend the truths. The basic facts that make or break our lives are grounded in plain truths.

II. Jesus Understands the Concerns of Humanity

A. He understands parents' concerns for their children.
1. In our text He understood the mothers' love for their children.
2. He understood a nobleman's heartache because of his son's illness (John 4:46-54).
3. He understood a Canaanite woman's heartache over her daughter's illness (Matt. 15:21-28).
4. Even following the marvelous experience of the Transfiguration, Jesus still cared about a parent's child (17:14-18).
5. Jesus cares about our children.
B. He understands our concerns for our friends. Illustration: He healed the paralyzed man whose friends brought him to Jesus (Mark 2).

III. Jesus Understands Life's Frustrations

A. He understood the confusion of the woman at the well (John 4). Life had mocked her. Jesus gave her hope.
B. He understood the hopelessness of the lepers (Luke 17:11-19). They were separated from their loved ones. He brought restoration.
C. He understood the disappointment that came with failure (John 21). The disciples were frustrated at having empty nets. Jesus filled the nets for them.
D. He understood Thomas's humanity (John 20:24-29). Jesus met him at the point of Thomas's need and helped his faith.

Conclusion

A. Jesus understands you and me. Sometimes life seems to make fun of our best efforts, but Jesus helps us to work through discouraging situations.
B. People may not understand us, but Jesus does. And that makes life worthwhile.

The Beauty of Jesus

1 Corinthians 10:23—11:1

Introduction
A. Read the scripture: 1 Cor. 10:23—11:1.
   1. This passage points out the freedom that we enjoy as believers.
   2. That freedom comes as a result of living for Jesus Christ.
B. In 1 Cor. 11:1 Paul is telling us that he followed Christ and so should we. Following Jesus results in beautiful things happening around us.

I. Wherever Jesus Went, Something Beautiful Happened
A. Look at some of the experiences in the scripture.
   1. As He passed through Jericho, a blind man began to see (Mark 10:46-52).
   2. As He passed by the Pool of Bethesda, a lame man walked (John 5:1-9).
   3. As He passed by Matthew, a selfish life took on new meaning (Matt. 9:9).
   4. As He passed by a cemetery in the land of the Gerasenes, a tormented man found peace (Mark 5).
   5. As He passed by Jacob's well, a hopeless woman was given new life (John 4).
   6. Everywhere He went, Jesus shared love, hope, strength, and a reason to enjoy life.
B. The ultimate aim of believers is that we, too, may communicate love, hope, and strength to those with whom we come into contact.
   1. We are to be like Him.
   2. When we live like Him, the world becomes interested in our experience.
C. Paul challenged the church at Corinth to live worthy of their name.

31

II. Some Things About Jesus That We Need to Remember

A. Jesus spread good news everywhere He went.
   1. His disciples never ceased to wonder at the gracious words He spoke.
   2. Jesus was not only good but also gracious to all people. This was one of the things that made Him so attractive to the people.
   3. Goodness is only effective when it is attractive. Graciousness makes it so.

B. Jesus reached out to everyone who came in contact with Him.
   1. He understood people and could, therefore, show sincere compassion to them.
   2. While His compassion was boundless, His sympathy was practical and personal.
   3. He expected people to help themselves. He did what they could not do.
   4. He was familiar with suffering but never encouraged self-pity.

C. Jesus loved people. Because of His keen insight He gave them what they needed.
   1. He always took time for people. He was never in a hurry.
   2. In just 3 1/2 years of ministry He still took time to get involved in people's lives.
   3. He had time to visit with a woman, hold children, and listen to lonely people.

D. The things that happened seemed to come about just because He was there.
   1. The nature of Jesus was to uplift the people with whom He came in contact.
   2. Everywhere He went, He did good things.

III. As followers of Jesus we emanate the beauty of His presence.

A. Somehow the grace and love of Jesus must reach out of our lives and touch those with whom we come in contact.
   1. As we concentrate on being like Him, the air that surrounds us will draw people we meet to Jesus.

2. Paul challenged us to be the aroma of Christ (2 Cor. 2:15).
B. Divine love needs to flow through us.
1. We must not live restricted lives that love only those who love us.
2. The love of Jesus cannot be self-contained. It must be unselfishly given.
C. The life of believers will radiate a lift to those who are around us.
D. The key to ministering as Jesus ministered is to fix our eyes on Him and let the love of Jesus flow through us to others.

Conclusion
A. As we live as Jesus lived, He passes by those with whom we come in contact, and they see His beauty.
B. Jesus said, "But I, when I am lifted up from the earth, will draw all men to myself" (John 12:32).

No Need for Alarm

John 21:1-13

Introduction

A. Our world lives on the edge of crisis. The threat of war in the Middle East hangs over us constantly. It seems that everything we eat or touch may cause cancer. The fear we will not receive our individual rights concerns many. Many other anticipated crises could be added to this list.

B. It is possible to be so preoccupied with potential crises that we become robbed of enjoying the things in our lives that are right. We have all of the freedom we could ever need to love each other. There are many opportunities to do noble work to help the lives of others. There are many good books we have not read. There is much joy to be found in the simple things of life—laughing with friends, catching a fish, holding a baby, and so on.

C. If life has become alarming and oppressive to you, it may be because you are not looking for joy in the right places. Jesus was the champion of simple, beautiful, pleasant experiences. Today's scripture illustrates the truth that we do not need to be alarmed. Read John 21:1-13. In a simple act of love, Jesus changed their day, and He can change ours too.

I. The First Step Toward Getting Help Is to Acknowledge Our Need (vv. 1-3)

A. The disciples had a real need and faced it openly.
1. They had put all of their trust in Jesus. The Crucifixion and Resurrection had created confusion among them.
2. So they sought help in a familiar experience—fishing.
3. That experience did not meet their need, but admitting their need brought help.

B. No one ever gets help until there is an acknowledgement of a problem.
1. Admitting there is a need is not weakness. It is a sign of a sound mind rather than a stubborn will.

2. Some people would die rather than go to a doctor, get a divorce rather than seek counseling, destroy someone rather than admit a mistake in judgment, go to hell rather than accept forgiveness, and so on.

II. The Second Step Is to Be in the Right Place— His presence (v. 4)

A. The disciples had cultivated the presence of Jesus. They did not know where He was at that particular time. Jesus knew where they were and that they needed Him.

B. People who practice being in His presence will experience His presence when they need Him.

1. I may not know where He is, but He always knows where I am.

2. Illustration: In poor visibility a pilot may not see the airport, but the air traffic controller has the plane on radar and can bring it to a safe landing.

3. Being in the presence of Jesus removes any reason to be afraid.

III. The Third Step Is Being Obedient to His Guidance (vv. 5-13)

A. The disciples' frustrations and fears were replaced with peace and plenty. They obeyed His command (v. 6). He knew their needs and prepared for them accordingly (vv. 10-13). Obedience was the catalyst between their need and His supply.

B. Today Jesus calls out to us much as He called the disciples. He does not want us to be afraid or frustrated. He will give guidance to everyone that will produce an abundant life. Those who are obedient to His call have no reason to be alarmed.

Conclusion

You are in the right place. Jesus is here. Recognize your need, and obey His command. Wherever you are in your life's journey, there is no need for alarm. There is help and hope that can be found in Jesus.

Welcome Home!

John 14:1-3

Introduction

A. This message comes from the closing moments of Jesus' life.

    1. He is preparing His disciples for His departure by promising them that the family of believers will be together again.

    2. Later He would give them the promise of usefulness (chap. 15), the promise of the Holy Spirit (chap. 16), and a prayer for unity (chap. 17).

    3. We need this same help today. We need to be useful, to have the Holy Spirit, to be unified, and to know that the family of believers will spend eternity together.

B. To be part of a family is a beautiful experience. An individual who is part of a loving, caring family is very fortunate. There is psychological stabilization for those who feel family support. When a happy family gets together, it is exciting. This is the way it should be in the church family—filled with times of happiness and support for each other.

C. Today's scripture gives us the assurance of peace in our hearts now and a future with the family of God. Read the scripture: John 14:1-3.

I. Jesus Gave Them a Plan of Support

A. Note His challenge in Verse 1.

    1. We are not to live with troubled hearts.

    2. We are to live with trust in our Heavenly Father and in Jesus.

B. What is Jesus saying in this verse?

    1. He is telling us that we are going to have some uncomfortable situations and times, but He is going to help us to get through all of them.

    2. Jesus promised a victorious outcome (16:33).

II. Jesus Promised a Place Would Be Prepared for Them

    A. That place would be one of fellowship, love, and peace. The words in the NIV, "many rooms," have been translated in numerous ways (14:2). But all translations reflect peace and assurance.

    B. The customary home of a wealthy person who lived in Israel at that time would fit the description that Jesus is giving here.

        1. Illustration: On the outskirts of Jericho are the ruins of a wealthy person's mansion that dates back to the time of Christ. It is the size of a football field with rooms around the entire perimeter and a great hall in the middle where the family ate and shared time together. Each child had equal access to the father and his provisions.

        2. This is the picture Jesus wants us to get. In eternity everyone will have equal access to the Father.

III. Jesus Promised a Great Family Reunion

    A. Jesus intends to get the family of believers together again (v. 3). In 12:26 He promises that where He is, His servants will be also. In 17:24 He prays to the Father for us to be where He is. Paul caught the spirit of the family reunion in 1 Thess. 4:15-18. Any way you interpret it, a homecoming is clearly promised for the people of God.

    B. The final homecoming will be a very special experience.

        1. Our Father will step into the center of the court of heaven with a voice as loud as thunder, clear as a trumpet, sweet as a psalm and say, "Welcome home, children."

        2. We are going to have a great homecoming feast (Rev. 19:9).

        3. There will be a great choir on that day (7:9-10).

        4. Following the concert we will get acquainted with family we may have never met.

Conclusion

Family gatherings on earth are always great times of fellowship. But we always have to leave them and go back to our homes. But on that final day when the family of God comes together, we will spend eternity together in the presence of our Father.

Jesus Simplified the Way

Matthew 22:34-40

Introduction

A. The Pharisees continuously looked for ways to entrap Jesus. They asked about paying taxes to Caesar (v. 15-22). They asked questions about marriage and the resurrection (v. 23-33). They finally asked which commandment was the greatest, to which Jesus responded with our text for the day. Read Matt. 22:34-40.

B. The worship routine of the Jews was a complicated series of rituals. There were so many laws concerning every area of life that no one could keep all of them. Some reports indicate that there were as many as 10,000 laws. Their laws became a form of bondage to them.

C. Jesus simplified the whole matter (vv. 37-39). He told them to love God and then do what comes naturally. He told them to love humankind and then do what comes naturally.

D. Sometimes we get too "hung up" on what is expected of us as Christians. We must have some physical guidelines. Illustration: Mention speed limits. We need spiritual guidelines to keep us within safe limits.

E. A mature experience with Jesus revolves around two simple statements of Jesus.

I. Love God

A. Love makes a difference in our attitude toward the object of our love. Illustration: When we fall in love, we do things that please the one we love. The same situation exists when we fall in love with God.

B. Love for God causes us to go beyond shallow religion. In our prayer life we not only talk to Him and listen to Him but also earnestly seek to find what is pleasing to Him. We read His Word, understanding that the Bible is God's love letter to us. We make the Lord's day a special day—not just a holiday but a holy day. We put Him first in every aspect of our lives. When contradictory paths arise, we choose the one He ordains.

C. All of the commandments relative to God are kept as the result of loving Him. All forms of service, tithing, and witnessing become natural to the person who loves God.

II. Love Humankind

A. In the same way that love for God makes it easy to keep the first four of the Ten Commandments, loving humankind enables us to keep the final six.

B. Love for our parents makes it easy to honor them.

C. We do not kill or wish death for those whom we love.

D. We do not commit an immoral act, because that would be murdering our emotions.
1. Adultery is the assassination of respect.
2. Committing adultery is a very selfish action.

E. We could never lie to or mislead someone we love.

F. We could never covet what others have when we love them. We are able to rejoice with them in their prosperity. Covetousness and selfishness are two peas in the same pod.

G. Rather than going down the list of God's moral laws, Jesus made it simple.

H. Keeping these two commands enables us to keep all 10 of the commandments that were given to Moses.

Conclusion

A. It is simple to be a Christian. We simply love God and do what comes naturally in that relationship. We love our neighbors as ourselves and do what comes naturally in that relationship.

B. Rituals, rules, and standards may all put meat on the bones of our Christian lives. But love is the foundation upon which we build.

C. We must get beyond the letter of the law in the realm of love, and our concept of Christianity will take on a new, deeper meaning.

D. Pleasing God is not complicated. Jesus made it simple.

The Sayings of Jesus

Matthew 7:24-29

Introduction

    A. Matthew's comment about the teachings of Jesus is important for us to remember.

        1. Read the scripture: Matt. 7:24-29.

        2. In the Sermon on the Mount Jesus spoke words that changed the lives of all who listened and heeded His advice.

        3. The same opportunity is available for us today.

    B. It is important to notice that Jesus gave many sayings that can make a difference in our lives if we listen to them and heed their messages.

I. Listen to Jesus' Words of Invitation (11:28-30)

    A. Jesus had just stated His position of power in the world (vv. 20-27).

        1. This could be frightening unless Verse 28 is attached.

        2. So that we will not be frightened away, He tenderly invites us to come to Him.

    B. Jesus says, "Come to me."

        1. He invites, but we must accept the invitation to enjoy His benefits.

        2. The invitation is to discover comfort and rest in His presence.

        3. We find another invitation in Rev. 22:17 that is desperately needed.

    C. Jesus said, "I will give you rest" (Matt. 11:28).

        1. Jesus is our "Noah," whose name signifies rest and safety.

        2. All who come to Jesus find freedom from weary, hopeless living.

II. Listen to Jesus' Words of Advice (6:33)

    A. Jesus had just spoken about the things humankind considers important.

1. Many people seek these things and become obsessed by them.
2. There are great values in the world, but Jesus urges us to seek the highest value.
B. God will always supply the needs of His people.
   1. What do we need that He does not possess in abundance?
   2. If we give Jesus first place in our lives, He takes responsibility for everything else.
C. We will never make a mistake in following Jesus' words of advice.

III. Listen to Jesus' Words of Direction (Mark 1:14-15)

A. Jesus had been in the wilderness, where He was tempted by Satan.
   1. While He was proving that He was victorious over Satan, John the Baptist had been imprisoned.
   2. Jesus knew His time had come to give words of guidance to people who wanted a relationship with the Father.
B. The Jews were looking for an uprising against Rome. Jesus was leading them to rise up against a very different power.
   1. They had broken God's law and needed grace.
   2. They needed to repent of their sins and experience a change in their lives.
C. Today by following Jesus' words of direction, our lives can be totally changed.

IV. Listen to Jesus' Words of Promise (John 6:34-37)

A. This is the one of the greatest promises of all.
   1. It gives us the promise of assurance and hope.
   2. It challenges us to seek His face.
B. Bread is the staff of life.
   1. Jesus is stating that He is the staff of life and anyone may come to Him.
   2. This is a clear invitation to leave all that competes with Him and come up to the standards upon which salvation is based.
C. This breaks down one of Satan's greatest arguments—that we cannot be saved.

1. He is saying that anyone can be saved.
2. Give an illustration of someone you know who has been delivered from sin by receiving the Bread of Life.

Conclusion

A. These sayings of Jesus can make an incredible difference in our lives.
1. They are words of invitation that lead us to comfort and strength.
2. They are words of advice that lead us to the best possible life.
3. They are words of direction to find peace with the Father.
4. They are words of promise that no one will be turned away.

B. Will you listen and respond to these words from the Master?

The Love of Jesus

Philippians 2:1-11

Introduction

A. It is impossible to recall any picture of Jesus Christ that is not focused on love. All of us have seen pictures of the Good Shepherd, Christ knocking at the door of our hearts, and Christ with a broken heart. We automatically think of love when we think of Jesus. That is as it should be.

B. Look at some displays of Jesus' nature. On occasion Jesus was stern, such as when He cleansed the Temple. He made no room for disobedience and sin. Note His admonition to the man He had healed at the pool of Bethesda in John 5:14.

C. Jesus was very strong physically. It was His strength that enabled Him to love others in spite of their imperfections. Weak people give up—loving only the lovable. Strong people love everyone. Jesus does not overlook our faults and failings. He "overloves" them.

D. In today's text, Paul challenges us to follow Jesus' example in our relationship with those around us. Read the scripture: Phil. 2:1-11.

I. Jesus taught love.

A. The great commandment is wrapped in love (Matt. 22:37). Jesus did not give a complicated list of rituals and ceremonies.

B. He made the second most important commandment to love those around us (v. 39). He even taught that we should love our enemies (5:44). Love covers faults and shortcomings and eliminates envy and jealousy. Loving those around us brings a wonderful dimension to our lives and enhances our Christian witness. We are not good followers of Jesus unless we practice what He taught—loving others as He first loved us.

43

II. Jesus Practiced Love

A. His life radiated love to those who knew Him best.

1. In describing the relationship between Lazarus and Jesus, John wrote, "Jesus loved Martha and her sister and Lazarus" (John 11:5). In verse 36 "the Jews said, 'See how he loved him!'"

2. On two occasions John referred to himself as "the disciple whom Jesus/he loved" (13:23 and 19:26).

3. In telling His disciples how He wanted them to live, Jesus said, "Love each other as I have loved you" (15:12).

B. Jesus even exhibited love to those who were apparent strangers. According to Mark 10:21, when a rich young man came to Him, "Jesus looked at him and loved him." His reaction to a crowd that constantly surrounded Him reflected His love. We can make an impact on our world today by demonstrating unconditional love to the people we meet.

III. Jesus' Ultimate Proof of His Love Was His Death on the Cross

A. The death of Jesus stated His message of love for the world. Paul spoke of the love of Christ in Gal. 2:20. Paul admonished the church and told of Jesus love (Eph. 5:2). In sacrificing His life for the world Jesus proved how much He loves everyone.

B. Today's text teaches one overwhelming lesson. Jesus loves you and me so much that He abandoned the luxury of heaven to hang on a rugged cross. He was with the Father and owed us nothing (Phil. 2:6). He stripped himself of His rights and privileges to come to earth (v. 7). He gave His life for you and me (v. 8).

C. The ultimate proof that we are followers of the Lord Jesus Christ is reflected in our lives when a love such as the love He demonstrated shines through us.

Conclusion

Our world is cold and impersonal in the way we treat each others. To Jesus each one of us is so special that He willingly paid the ultimate price. Jesus loves you. Will you respond to that love?

TRIED AND TRIUMPHANT

James 1:12; Matthew 4:1-11

Introduction

A. There are many places in the Bible where God endeavors to relieve Christians from the anxiety that comes as a result of temptation. Many people misunderstand temptation and are defeated by it. We must understand that temptation itself is not sin. Trials and temptations are opportunities for triumphant living (James 1:12).

B. Read the scripture passage from Matt. 4:1-11. Jesus was tempted in every way just as we are (Heb. 4:15). By taking a better look at the temptations of Jesus we can gain strength that will help us when we are faced with temptation.

I. Look at the Source of Temptation

A. The temptations of Jesus address the major weaknesses to Christian living.
   1. The temptation of Jesus came immediately after His baptism (Matt. 3:13-17).
   2. Our most severe temptations may come after mountaintop experiences.
   3. Illustration: A pendulum swings from one extreme to the other.

B. Notice the temptation to doubt (4:3, 6).
   1. Most temptation comes when the wedge of doubt begins to separate us from our confidence in God.
   2. Illustration: In the same way that we can use a steel wedge to split logs, Satan tries to use doubt to separate us from God.
   3. Once Satan gets us to doubt, he has the upper hand.

C. Notice the temptation to gratify the physical appetites (vv. 2 and 3).
   1. Christ had fasted 40 days. When the fast was over, He was hungry.
   2. Satan attacked Him at His weakest point.

3. We are highly susceptible to physical temptations because we think they are normal.
4. Satan takes legitimate things and tempts us to use them in illegitimate ways that lead to sin.

D. Notice the temptation to seek praise of others (vv. 5-6). This was a logical point of temptation for Jesus, since He came to win the world. This is a logical point of temptation for us because we want people to like us.

E. Notice the temptation to seek personal gain (vv. 8-9).
1. Jesus had come to gain the world, but He paid for it with His life.
2. Satan promises that which he cannot deliver.

II. Look at the Formula for the Triumphant

A. It is not enough to know Satan will tempt us. We must know how to face him.
1. The first step toward victory is to know who we are and what our assignment is. Jesus did.
2. Victory comes when we realize that our primary assignment is to glorify God and not ourselves.

B. Look at Jesus' formula.
1. He recognized who the enemy was—Satan.
2. Jesus used His knowledge of the Old Testament as His major weapon in defeating Satan (vv. 4, 7, 10).
3. It is important to be well grounded in the Scriptures. David wrote, "I have hidden your word in my heart that I might not sin against you" (Ps. 119:11).
4. Jesus stood firm as He battled Satan. While we should not subject ourselves to temptation, when temptations come, we do not need to run (1 Cor. 10:13).
5. Jesus kept in view His real assignment, which was to glorify the Father by redeeming humankind.
6. We must keep in mind that our major assignment is to glorify our Father by reflecting His love to everyone we encounter.

Conclusion

A. After Jesus withstood the temptations, notice what happened in Matt. 4:11. Satan fled and angels attended Him.
B. If we follow Jesus' formula, we will have the same experience today.

JOY FOR THE JOURNEY

John 15:9-17

Introduction

   A. The last night of His life, Jesus prepared the disciples to carry on His work. He gave them an example of humility (chap. 13). He gave them hope for the future (chap. 14). He gave them an assignment to fulfill while they waited (chap. 15). He gave them an explanation of how they would carry on (chap. 16). He prayed for their unity as believers (chap. 17).

   B. Right in the midst of this, Jesus spoke to one of the greatest needs—joy. Read John 15:9-17. Genuine joy is one of the most attractive traits of Christianity. Fun is dependent upon physical conditions. Happiness is the result of an internal condition. Joy is the condition that results from knowing that our lives are under His control.

   C. Today we are focusing on having joy for the journey of life. Christlike people have joy that causes happiness that enables us to have fun. It is a joy that shines like headlights in a dark, dangerous world.

I. Take a Good Look at the Joy Jesus Experienced

   A. He came into the world to carry out His Father's will. Note Jesus' response to His disciples. "My food . . . is to do the will of him who sent me and to finish his work" (John 4:31-34). His satisfaction came from carrying out His Father's will.

   B. Jesus built a bridge between God and humankind so that we can enjoy His presence. Separation can cause loneliness and sorrow. Because of Jesus, we do not have to be separated from our Father. The Cross is our bridge to fellowship with our Father.

   C. Look at Jesus' life. He enjoyed a party (Matt. 9:11). Children were attracted to Him (Mark 10:13-16).

   D. People are attracted to joyful experiences. Illustration: Who was ever attracted to joining a funeral procession?

Many people crash parties because of the fun that is happening.

II. How Do We Find a Joy Like Jesus Experienced?

    A. This comes by having absolute faith in God.

        1. The level of our pleasure in life will be in direct ratio to our faith in His Word.

        2. We can trust Him with the stuff that others struggle with (Prov. 3:5-6).

    B. This also comes when we make a total commitment to His will. See Isa. 1:19 and Jer. 29:11.

        1. Jesus prayed in the garden, "Yet not my will, but yours be done" (Luke 22:42).

        2. The Father's will resulted in Jesus' crucifixion. But He was also resurrected.

        3. We may have uncomfortable experiences, but when we get to the other side, we will find incredible joy.

        4. Illustration: Children feel free when traveling with their parents. In that same way we can feel free as we travel through life with our Father.

III. God Intended for Life to be a Joyful Journey

    A. We must remember who our traveling companion is.

        1. Our companion is the One who created the world and has limitless resources.

        2. He is the same One who is so powerful that He has never lost a battle.

        3. He is the same One who loved us enough to die for us.

    B. Joy for the journey does not come from just being religious. Illustration: Tell the story of the rich young man (Mark 10:17-23).

    C. God wants each of us to enjoy life's journey. Jesus did, and so can we.

Conclusion

Do the people with whom you interact see enough joy in your life to want to join you on your journey?

The Difference the Master Makes

Mark 5:1-17

Introduction
A. It is always amazing to notice the difference Jesus makes in people.
   1. Many times the change is so miraculous that people have trouble believing it.
   2. One of the reasons Jesus came was to lift our lives to a higher level.
B. Our scripture for today is a classic case of the difference He makes. Read the scripture: Mark 5:1-17.

I. The First Truth Revolves Around the Community's Response (vv. 14-17)
A. The people asked Jesus to leave.
   1. It didn't seem to matter to them that their neighbor had been healed from a lifelong illness.
   2. It didn't seem to matter to them that they could travel in their neighborhood without fear.
   3. The community demonstrated a horrible sense of values.
   4. It seemed to mean nothing to them that their neighbor was "sitting there, dressed and in his right mind" (v. 15b).
B. This is an example of the poor sense of values that exists in many places today.
   1. Money and material possessions are more important than human life and dignity.
   2. Much of our world has bowed to the gods of materialism. As a result, we pay a high price in human misery.
   3. In defense of the Gerasenes, perhaps they were afraid because they did not understand how this miracle had happened.
   4. They should have looked at the results and rejoiced that a neighbor and a neighborhood were at peace.
C. The values of much of today's society have created an out-of-control situation.

1. Sometimes when someone tries to respond to the misery, some take the attitude, "Give us our pigs."
2. We may not be able to open the eyes of that crowd because there are none so blind as those who will not see.

II. The Second Truth Is One We Can Do Something About

A. In reality, this truth is the main message of the story. Regardless of how messed up a person's life may be, Jesus can change it (vv. 3-5).
B. The series of negatives in these verses indicates that the man was unmanageable.
   1. His life appeared to be totally ruined.
   2. The good news is that no one is too far gone for Jesus' grace to reach them.
   3. Illustration: The life of John Newton, a drunken sailor, was changed. He wrote the song, "Amazing Grace."
C. It is amazing what can be done when the right power and ability get to the point of need.
   1. Many have tried for years to make something meaningful of their lives. Jesus can do just that.
   2. Jesus wants to help each of us because He loves us.
D. There is no one present who is bound by the chains of any sinful habits that Jesus cannot break.
   1. There are no new sins.
   2. Jesus has already done for others what needs to be done in all of our lives.

Conclusion

A. There are people present today whose lives have been totally transformed by the power of God.
   1. There are others present who need the touch and deliverance that Jesus can bring.
   2. The Master is here and can bring freedom to all and restore value to their lives.
B. Come to Jesus. Let Him make a difference in your life today by setting you free from the chains that bind you.

DELIGHTING GOD

Matthew 17:1-5

Introduction

A. The transfiguration of Jesus was a very special experience for those who were privileged to be witnesses.
   1. Jesus had been in the Galilee area for many days. Many things had happened. 5,000 people had been fed with a lad's lunch (John 6). A Canaanite woman's daughter had been healed (Matt. 15). Jesus had walked on water (John 6).
   2. Jesus had come back to the western shore of the Sea of Galilee to Magdala. The Pharisees began to argue about signs and to question His authority. Jesus wanted to make sure the disciples had a clear understanding of who He was. As they walked north toward Caesarea Philippi, Jesus asked them, "Who do you say I am?" (Matt. 16:15). Jesus took Peter, James, and John to the top of the mount for a special experience.
   3. Read the scripture: Matt. 17:1-5.
B. In this confirmation by the Father there is a very important statement. It is important to note the confirmation of Christ's divinity in this passage. He was not only divine; Jesus was a delight to His Heavenly Father (v. 5b).
C. As Christians we must live in such a way that we are not just saved but also pleasing to our Heavenly Father.
   1. The Father was "wonderfully pleased" (TLB).
   2. Our greatest accomplishment is to live in such a way that our Heavenly Father is wonderfully pleased with our lives.
D. How do we make sure of this?
   1. We let the beauty of Jesus shine through our lives.
   2. We need to look at three characteristics of Jesus that enable us to delight our Heavenly Father.

I. Jesus Lived in Positive Confidence

A. The Father had sent Him into the world with power, and

He used it. All of the miracles are expressions of His confidence in the Father's provision. Illustration: Note John 11:41-42: "Father, I thank you that you have heard me." It is interesting to note that Jesus did not exploit His position with the Father. He just lived expecting things to happen.

B. How are you living? It pleases the Father when we live displaying our confidence in Him. The Father is delighted when we live positively in the midst of trying situations.

II. Jesus Lived in Total Obedience to His Father

A. We are well aware of Jesus' prompt obedience to the Father's will.

1. Our thoughts go immediately to Gethsemane. "Yet not as I will, but as you will" (Matt. 26:39b).
2. When Jesus taught His followers to pray, He taught them to respect the Father's will. "Your will be done on earth as it is in heaven" (6:10).
3. A casual statement from John 4:34 is enlightening. "My food . . . is to do the will of him who sent me."

B. As parents, we are pleased when our children obey us. So is our Heavenly Father.

III. Jesus Lived a Life of Love for Humankind

A. His love was so obvious that those looking on took note of it. It was evident at Lazarus's death (John 11:36). When Jesus saw the crowds, His love moved Him (Matt. 9:36). When He saw the rich young man, He loved Him (Mark 10:21). The atmosphere that surrounded Jesus was one of warmth and loving compassion.

B. Jesus encouraged us to love one another (John 13:34). We cannot experience the beauty of Jesus without loving each other.

Conclusion

A. The Father was well pleased with Jesus because He believed Him, obeyed Him, and loved His highest creation.

B. God is pleased when the beauty of Jesus shines through our lives.

HE IS COMING

Matthew 25:1-13

Introduction

A. In recent years there has been a surge of interest in the return of Jesus Christ. Millions of books on this subject have been sold in recent years. Much study and discussion has taken place on the events surrounding the second coming of Jesus Christ.

B. Through the years many have speculated about when and how Jesus will return. Many have set dates and led naive people into believing false predictions.

C. The Bible is very clear in its statement found in Matt. 25:13.

D. There is one thing about which there is no speculation. Jesus is coming again. The Bible is very clear in the statements regarding His return. See Acts 1:11; 1 Thess. 4:16; Heb. 9:28; and 1 John 3:2. Jesus promised to return. See Matt. 24:29-30; 26:64; and John 14:1-3.

E. The Bible has over twice as much to say about the Second Coming than it does in the promise of the initial advent of the Messiah.

1. If we believe the Bible is true, we must believe that Jesus is coming again.

2. If we believe that Jesus was a good man, we must believe He is coming again as He promised.

3. Today's scripture is a parable that Jesus gave to teach about His return. Read the scripture: Matt. 25:1-13.

I. Look at the Results of Jesus Coming

A. Those who are not ready for His return will face the ultimate disaster.

1. They will be separated forever from the love of God (2 Thess. 1:9).

2. They will pay the price of eternal punishment (v. 9).

B. Those who are ready will experience eternal joy.

1. Their long wait will be over.

      2. The joy experienced at Jesus' birth will not compare with the joy that will be experienced in heaven.

      3. Look at this scripture: Rev. 7:13-17; 21:3-4; 22:1-5.

  C. Illustration: When soldiers come home from war, families celebrate. We have received word that Jesus is coming.

II. Look at the Parable Jesus Gives in the Text (Matt. 25:1-13)

  A. In this parable, Jesus gives us important lessons about His return.

      1. Everything in the context of this passage makes it very clear that Jesus is talking about His second coming.

      2. He warned that the time would arrive unexpectedly and find many unprepared.

      3. Before and after this parable He spoke of wise servants who performed their duties while the master was away as well as unwise servants who were careless in their conduct (see Matt 24:45-51; 25:14-31).

  B. Looking deeper at this parable we discover the following (25:1-13).

      1. It is very clear that the bridegroom is Jesus.

      2. The occasion of Jesus' coming is a joyous marriage feast.

  C. The foremost lesson of the parable is to "keep watch because [we] do not know the day or the hour" (v. 13).

  D. The people involved were not ungodly or immoral. They were simply careless. The wise ones paid the price to be prepared at any moment.

  E. The separation was permanent (vv. 10-12).

III. The Lessons Jesus Gave Us Are Very Clear

  A. Jesus Christ, our King of Kings, is coming again.

  B. The exact time of His coming is totally unpredictable.

  C. Waiting is not sufficient. We must be prepared to enter in at all times.

  D. Being good is not enough (See 7:21).

Conclusion

  A. Once Jesus has returned and the opportunity has been missed, no further arrangements can be made.

  B. The essential question is not "Will He come?" or "When will He come?" but "Will you be ready when He comes?"

Follow Me

Matthew 16:24-28

Introduction

A. The life that is pleasing to God is not found in a series of religious duties. Rather, it is found in obedience.

    1. Illustration: Parents are happy when their children are obedient and follow the family guidelines. Happy parents have happy children.

    2. According to Isa. 1:19 God feels this same way about us.

        a. It is not our activities that please God (vv. 13-15).

        b. He is pleased by our obedience (v. 19).

    3. The hallmark of obedience is joy.

B. Today we are looking at a very powerful but simple truth from God's Word.

    1. Read the scripture: Matt. 16:24-28.

    2. This passage runs counter to the self-centered teaching of today's society.

    3. It points out very clearly the options that are available to us.

I. There Is a Decision We Must Make

A. Jesus said, "If anyone would come after me, he must deny himself" (v. 24). This phrase is pregnant with meaning. Jesus is asking us if we want to be where He is.

B. The decision is not complicated.

    1. We must decide if we want to be identified with Jesus.

        a. Do I want to be His friend?

        b. The disciples had to evaluate their relationship with Jesus. Not everyone looked upon Him with favor.

    2. Today, our decision is simple. Do we want to be identified with Jesus?

    3. We are faced with a moment of truth.

II. There Is a Price to be Paid

A. The cost of paying the price means self-denial (v. 24).

1. While grace is free to us, it was expensive for Jesus.
2. Since our salvation cost Him so much, it must cost us something to belong to Him.
3. Jesus is very open about the cost of following Him. There is no hidden cost.
4. Illustration: Some automobile ads are misleading. They do not tell you about hidden costs.

B. The scripture says, "He must deny himself" (v. 24).
   1. The NEB translates this as, "Leave self behind."
   2. This is totally counter to the attitude of our day.

C. "Let him . . . take up his cross" (v. 24, KJV).
   1. This statement has been abused by much shallow thinking. It has been interpreted to relate to hard times that come our way.
   2. It means "death to self." Paul writes, "I have been crucified with Christ" (Gal. 2:20). We must carry our cross to our Calvary.

D. This is a vital area for triumphant Christian living.
   1. Self-centered love and Christ are not compatible.
   2. When we turn loose of self and seek Him, we experience the joy of great freedom (John 8:36).

III. We Have an Example to Follow

A. As Christians we must follow the lifestyle of Jesus.
   1. Since He was not self-conscious, He was able to reach out to others.
   2. Jesus was authentic. He was and is what He appeared to be.

B. Heaven is the wonderful destination for everyone who follows Jesus.
   1. The instructions are clear and simple. Jesus tells us that if we follow Him, we will be where He is.
   2. We do not have to figure it out. We simply follow Him.

Conclusion

A. The word *follow* is a command.
B. Obedient people have a wonderful eternity with Jesus.

THE RISEN JESUS—THE CURE

Luke 24:13-49

Introduction

A. This passage is from the post-Resurrection period of the New Testament. The truth that Jesus Christ is alive became an established fact.

B. Jesus was resurrected, but God knew the skeptical minds of humankind. He validated the miracle of our risen Savior.

1. He could have taken Jesus away and left people who had strong faith as believers. But others would have questioned Jesus' resurrection.

2. God determined that we should have every help possible in accepting Jesus as Savior. That is why He provided 40 days for Jesus' appearances.

C. In establishing the truth of the Resurrection, God gave us several lessons that were needed then and are still needed today. Read the scripture: Luke 24:13-49.

I. Lesson No. 1: Jesus Is the Cure for Sorrow

A. Look at Jesus' appearance on the road to Emmaus (vv. 13-32). In Verse 17 we read that they were sad and filled with sorrow. Jesus came and brought new meaning to their lives. They could not put together the shattered pieces of their hopes and dreams. But Jesus did (v. 32). In Verse 35 we read that doubts and sorrow have gone. The risen Lord has come!

B. This experience is a reality today. Jesus was not a cure for sorrow only in biblical days. He still is today. Grieving is not wrong. But there is a cure—the presence of Jesus.

II. Lesson No. 2: Jesus Is the Cure for Confusion

A. Look at Jesus' appearance to the disciples and other believers (vv. 36-43). They had been through some very heartbreaking experiences. Their minds were reeling. They could not be sure of what was happening. Look at verse 37. Jesus gave them some concrete evidence (v. 39). To clear up all of their doubts, He gave them more evidence (vv. 41-43). Satan raised doubts, but Jesus cured their confusion with His presence.

B. Jesus is still the author of confidence and cure for confusion. While many voices speak out in our day, an experience with Him eliminates all of the questions on every issue of importance. Jesus is not confusing. He is the cure for society's questions and condition.

III. Lesson No. 3: Jesus Is the Cure for Fear

A. The disciples were afraid (v. 37).
  1. In John 20:19 we read, "The disciples were together, with the doors locked for fear of the Jews."
  2. They had a right to be afraid. They had witnessed the brutal treatment of Jesus.
  3. Put yourself in their situation, and you must acknowledge that you would be afraid too. They did not know who might be taken next.
  4. Jesus came to them and offered peace (Luke 24:36).
  5. John made note of this same greeting in 20:19.
  6. If Jesus had not come to them and cured their fear, they would not have survived.
  7. Jesus came and gave them directions for receiving God's power (v. 49). They obeyed, and as a result, they shook their world.

B. Jesus is still the cure for fear today. He promised and produced victory (John 16:33). This means Jesus is greater than any difficulty we will ever face (1 John 4:4).

IV. Lesson No. 4: Jesus Is the Cure for Sin

A. Jesus went to Calvary to pay the price for our sins. Heb. 9:14 makes this lesson very clear.

B. It was for the forgiveness of not only New Testament Christians but us as well.

Conclusion

Because Jesus lives, we can face life and anything that comes our way. The risen Jesus is the cure.

The Amazing Master

Mark 4:35-41

Introduction
A. Jesus amazed everyone who ever met Him.
   1. It was hard for some of them to believe the miracle of His birth, but there He was.
   2. The teachers in the Temple were amazed at the wisdom that came from the young Jesus as He answered their questions.
   3. The Sermon on the Mount astonished the people as He taught simple truths.
   4. The miracles He performed constantly amazed the multitudes as they saw startling things happen.
   5. His patience at His trial surprised those who were trying Him. Jesus was the perfect picture of peace (Matt. 27).
   6. There is something magnetic about Jesus. He is different from anyone else that we have ever met.
B. The most amazing thing of all is that Jesus loves you and me.
   1. Because of His love we can have a personal experience with Him.
   2. Enormous strength comes to us through this intimate relationship with Him.
C. The fourth and fifth chapters of Mark highlight areas in people's lives where Jesus brought great victory.
D. Read the scripture: Mark 4:35-41.

I. Jesus Gives Us the Strength to Overcome Danger from Without
A. Jesus and the disciples were caught in a fierce storm on the Sea of Galilee.
   1. The sudden storms that sweep over the mountains can be frightening experiences.
   2. The disciples were afraid for their lives and awakened Jesus (v. 38).

3. He showed then that He cared by delivering them from danger (v. 39).
4. The disciples were amazed at His power (v. 41).
   B. Jesus still provides amazing strength for His followers.
1. We can be sure that some furious storms will come into our lives.
2. They are not always physical things. Sometimes other aspects of our lives can be very frightening to us.
3. Jesus still helps believers in times of need.

II. Jesus Can Give Us Strength to Overcome Dangers from Within (Mark 5:19-20)

A. Jesus had an encounter with a man who lived in a cemetery.
1. The problem in this case was not with pressure from without but within.
2. Satan can fill a person's heart until he or she loses all sense of control.
3. Notice how much evil can dwell in a person's heart (v. 13).
4. Notice how much peace Jesus can give (v. 15).
5. They were amazed at what Jesus had done.
B. People in our world still have internal problems.
1. Some people are miserable within themselves.
2. This makes it extremely difficult to have healthy relationships with others.
3. Jesus is able to bring inner calm and peace to troubled hearts,

III. Jesus Can Give Us the Strength to Overcome Physical Problems (vv. 24-34)

A. The woman in this passage had a serious physical problem.
1. Luke wrote that no physician could help her (Luke 8:43).
2. Jesus healed her in response to her faith.
3. The disciples were amazed that He became so involved (Mark 5:31).
B. Jesus still has the power to deliver us from physical problems when it is His will.

IV. Jesus can give us victory in times of sorrow (vv. 22-24, 35-43)

    A. Notice the interest Jesus displays in the individuals in this passage.

        1. He met them at the point of their need.

        2. He did what needed to be done to help the broken-hearted people.

        3. The people looking on were amazed (v. 42).

    B. Jesus still gives victory in the hour of death.

        1. Sometimes He delivers a person from the hand of death.

        2. When death comes, He gives peace and victory to the bereaved (Ps. 23:4).

        3. Paul wrote that the sting of death is gone (1 Cor. 15:55).

Conclusion

    A. We can understand why people were amazed at Jesus. He was the Master of every situation.

    B. The most amazing thing of all is that Jesus is the same today (Heb. 13:8).

The Purpose of His Coming

John 3:14-17

Introduction

A. Many people have the wrong conception of what it means to be a Christian.
1. They consider Christianity solely from a negative aspect.
2. The positives of being a Christian overshadow anything that seems negative.
3. A Christian can do anything that is honest, clean, moral, loving, and kind.

B. The main reason Jesus came into the world was to provide freedom and joy.
1. Read the scripture: John 3:14-17.
2. Jesus made this very clear when He said, "I have come that they may have life, and have it to the full" (10:10*b*).

I. Jesus Was Lifted Up So That We Could Be Safe (John 3:14)

A. Moses lifted the serpent in the wilderness for the safety of the people.
1. The brass serpent was their only hope for deliverance (Num. 21:5-9).
2. It was a voluntary exercise of faith for the people to look and live.

B. Jesus set people free from the serpent's, Satan's, bite.
1. He delivered Mary Magdalene from demons (Luke 8:2).
2. He delivered Zacchaeus from a miserable life (Luke 19).
3. He delivered the woman at the well from her sinful lifestyle (John 4).
4. Jesus did not cast them out as hopeless cases. He set them free.

C. Today, Jesus still will set all people free if they will look to Him for help.

1. Deliverance from the chains of sin is still based on a voluntary response.
2. Like the children of Israel in Num. 21, deliverance is provided for us.

II. For Whom Was Jesus Lifted Up? (John 3:15-16)

A. He was raised up for each one of us individually.
   1. While the serpent was lifted up for all the people, it took a personal response of each individual to experience deliverance.
   2. Each one of us must respond personally if we are ever to know freedom from sin.
   3. Simply being reared in a Christian environment is not adequate for deliverance.

B. In this passage we read that everyone is included.
   1. In Verse 15 we read, "Everyone who believes." In Verse 16 we read, "Whoever believes." That makes it clear that all who believe can experience His grace.
   2. Jesus earnestly seeks to save every person (2 Peter 3:9).
   3. Jesus said, "Whoever comes to me I will never drive away" (John 6:37).

C. The Bible makes it clear. Jesus came into the world to save everyone who wants to have a relationship with his or her Heavenly Father.

III. We Find the True Purpose for Which Jesus Came in (John 3:17)

A. Jesus' primary mission was not to condemn but to save.
   1. Illustration: Tell about the woman caught in the act of adultery (chap. 8).
   2. When the blind man was healed, His disciples asked Him who had sinned. Jesus responded that no one had sinned (John 9).
   3. While sin destroys and degrades, Jesus spent His life lifting people up.

B. It is clear that Jesus came into the world to save us from our sins.
   1. "For God did not send his Son into the world to condemn the world, but to save the world through him" (3:17).

2. Jesus does not destroy the joy of life, but rather He enriches our lives.
3. Illustration: People who do not know Jesus are living beneath their privilege. This is like Bill Gates, one of the richest men in the world, moving into the slums.

Conclusion

A. John makes a very significant statement in Verse 17. "For God did not send the Son into the world in order to judge—to reject, to condemn, to pass sentence on—the world; but that the world might find salvation and be made safe and sound *through* Him" (AMP., emphasis added).
   1. There is no other one to whom we can go to enjoy this experience.
   2. To save the lost is the reason why Jesus came into the world.
B. The success of His coming is dependent upon our having the faith to look to Jesus and live. Will you take advantage of that opportunity today?